The Better Things in Life Await You

By

Mary Ellen Davis

The Better Things in Life Await You by Mary Ellen Davis

The Better Things in Life Await You
Mary Ellen Davis
ISBN 13: 978-0615870472
ISBN 10: 0615870473

Published by Parablist Publishing House, Inc.
www.parablistbooksonline.com
Email: parablistpublishing@yahoo.com

Table of Contents

A Note from the Author

At the time I thought about writing this book, I was working at Ann J. Kellogg School as a Foster Grandparent. I worked with children from K through sixth grade. I taught them reading, arithmetic, and read them stories which they loved very much. I taught them how to love others and be respectful and kind to the elderly. If you teach children these things while they are young, they will mostly keep them in their minds and not forget them. We learned how to play lots of different games together. Working with the children made me feel much younger and more active. They loved for me to work with them and I enjoyed working with them. Children are a lot of fun.

I have had students come to me since they graduated from high school to thank me for teaching them how to read. Reading is one of the most important things to learn. First you learn to read, and then, you read to learn! It is hard for some youngsters to learn to read, so it takes one on one work with them, being kind and patient with them. I loved working with the boys and girls because it's a challenge for me. We need them in our lives, and they need us. They teach us as well as we teach them. It was a pleasure for me to be a Foster Grandparent. I loved working with the teachers and they were all so kind. The principal did such a wonderful job at that school. She was loved by everyone.

The Better Things in Life Await You by Mary Ellen Davis

Before we go further into this book, I must tell you about my life. I became a foster grandparent in the year of 1991. I have been a Foster Grandparent for many, many years.

My love for the children was what led me to write my life story. I hope that by sharing my life story young people will be inspired to grow in knowledge and appreciate life, and maximize opportunities to get the most out of it. I hope that by comparing my life story with things as they know them, it will be an exciting, eye-opening challenge for them.

I decided to share my story so that boys and girls would be able to read it and perhaps find some good tips that will help shape their lives in the future. In this book, I tell my story of being a little girl born and raised on the farm. Through my story, you learn a lot about life and different things in life on the farm. I hope my story will help you with lessons you (children) can use to enjoy the fabulous future that awaits you.

Dedication

To all little children growing up to be the best you can be.

To the boys and girls that might grow up and lose interest on the way.

*I especially dedicate this story to children who are struggling and feel afraid to ask for help. A "Grandparent" can be found who will encourage and help you.
Don't give up.*

This little story is for all of you who will take the time to read it.

*Thanks to the former Principal of Ann J. Kellogg School,
for giving me encouraging words about doing this.*

A School to be Remembered

Ann J. Kellogg School is a very important school to me because I have a son who attended this school when he was young. He is disabled with Cerebral Palsy. He had no use of his right arm, one leg was shorter than the other, no use of his right side, and he experienced many seizures, sometimes, more than one per day.

Two wonderful nurses worked at the school, whom I called "Miracle Workers". They were the kind of people that gave their all and all. They were very concerned about all of the students.

Two of them kept pleading for my son to have surgery so he could use his right hand as a "helper". They were sure it would make a difference. Finally, the surgery was done.

Today, my son is able to use his right hand as a helper.

All of these things happened because of the wonderful type of school Ann J. Kellogg School is. They have the right teachers with the expertise, knowledge and tender loving care to address students' needs. This is a school where one never feels left out. Someone is always willing to help you or find the right resources to help you.

In spite of Doctors saying that my son would never "make it", he did.

The Better Things in Life Await You by Mary Ellen Davis

My son graduated with an Associates Degree in Business Management from Kellogg Community College and worked with his dad in electronics.

Thanks be to God for giving Teachers the knowledge to care enough to do a wonderful job!

Acknowledgements

Thanks to Mrs. Gloria Robertson, the former Principal of Ann J. Kellogg Elementary School, for the encouragement she gave me to write this book.

Mrs. Robertson took the time when I was a Foster Grandparent to notice the work I did with the children K-6. She thought enough about my work to inspire me to write a book. With her inspiration and the love I have for the children, I have written this book.

I would like to thank Cheryl Roberts for introducing me to the Foster Grand Parent Program. I owe a huge thank you to my daughter, Simmie Marie Davis for helping to get my book published. We have been on this journey together.

Special thanks to George Martinez, an artist from Battle Creek, Michigan for his charcoal drawings included in this book. Special thanks to Jean Van Atta colorist, for the charcoal pictures included in this book of Green Street Studios. Also, thank you goes out to those who had a hand in helping me with distribution, PR and everything else needed to get this book published; Tim Elliott, Gwendolyn Bodiford and countless other family and friends who encourage me to keep on believing and writing.

The Better Things in Life Await You by Mary Ellen Davis

11
The Better Things in Life Await You by Mary Ellen Davis

Chapter One

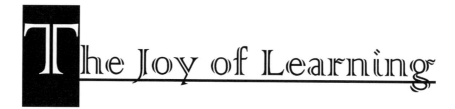

I was born in a little town in Texas with a German name. It was called Malakoff. I attended school, in a small community five miles away, called Saint Paul High School. It was a boarding school. I came from a family of thirteen children. There were eight girls and five boys.

I once was a little person just like you are today. I loved going to school. I would cry when I couldn't go to school. I thought going to school was the coolest thing you could do. My mother would make our little dresses out of the sacks that we bought flour in. They were of all colors, and we got a chance to choose our own colors. We had to wait for a while to get our dresses, but it was worth the wait. My mother made little bow ties in the back of our dresses.

I thought I looked so good in my little dresses. I would get up in the morning, and of course do all of my chores, (the things my parents wanted us to do), and then eat my breakfast. It is very important to eat breakfast. After breakfast, I would get ready for school, and off we would go.

The Better Things in Life Await You by Mary Ellen Davis

14

The Better Things in Life Await You by Mary Ellen Davis

We started working and doing chores, milking cows and riding horses early in life. I was born and raised on a large farm, which meant we always had a lot of work to do. We enjoyed doing our work on the farm. We would milk the cows by hand, we did not have electric milkers in those days, we would take the cows to the pastures, then go get them in the afternoon and milk them again. This was fun, because we could ride the horses to round up the cattle, just like a cowboy (smile). We had to keep their stalls really clean also.

You see, boys and girls, I always wanted to be somebody. For me, being somebody meant growing up to be a schoolteacher, nurse, music teacher or something like that.

As I grew older, I found out that I was already somebody, but I needed to get an education so I wouldn't have to depend on other people for every thing I wanted to do. We must learn to think for ourselves and be able to get a good paying job so we can plan our future and be independent.

We need to learn math so that we won't get cheated out of our money and other things. We need to learn to read so that we can keep up with what's going on. We need to learn to write so that we can write our checks and sign our name and many other things.

You need to fill your brain with all you can while you are young, because now you can learn it, and retain it. It will be stored in your little memory book, "The Brain" for good. There is nothing like studying hard and learning all you can. Learning is such a great asset in your life.

The first school I went to was a boarding school. A boarding school then meant that each student who needed to, lived in that school. Each student worked in the school to pay for them staying there. This training school focused on the Performing Arts. This came in handy when a tornado hit our school. We had to use our talents to raise money for our school. to get fixed and stay open.

In boarding school, I learned how to be a good dancer. Tap dancing was my favorite. I also learned how to be an actor. I enjoyed being on the stage in front of people; acting out a part of a song I would be singing. Tap dancing gave me exercise.

School is not hard; it is a joy because you have the freedom to learn, freedom to be with other boys and girls, and learn all about them. Freedom to go to school, sit and think about things and learn a variety of different things.

17

When I was growing up, we did not get into a lot of fighting and fooling around. We were too glad to be with one another, and share our thoughts. We knew that a big wide future was before us, and we needed to equip ourselves to compete with it. We wanted to be all that we could be and be fully equipped.

In today's world, being fully prepared is one thing needed to survive in this world. There was a time when you could get by with a little education, but you can't do that anymore. Today's world is equipped with computers and all of this new technology. If you don't learn it, you will find yourself left out.

You must fill your mind with knowledge, not just the fun things. You must not let people lead you into wrong things; it will only ruin your life and drag you down. There is nothing that can compare to being looked up to and being well thought of.

It is so precious to have a good life. You can be very happy. When I was growing up, we did not have the luxury of owning a lot of things to entertain us as you have today.

Giving Thanks!

By Re'Zon

For fun we played lots of jacks. We also made horses out of grasshoppers.

Horses (Grasshoppers)

We made rag dolls, paper doll clothes using corn silks for doll hair and corn shucks for the body. We made jigsaw puzzles out of string and a lot of other little things you probably wouldn't think of today.

Today, it is so wonderful that you don't have to make your own toys. You have television, basketball courts and baseball diamonds and fields and many different types of recreational places. Take advantage of these things and don't let them pass you by.

When I was in school, we had spelling bees, and I would always be a part of that. At times, I did very well. I played in the school band and I was in acrobatics, and I played basketball.

In elementary school, I was a majorette. I loved to sing and act on the stage. The school would travel to a lot of places and I would be on stage and sing and act out my songs. We were often on the radio. I also played the piano during those years.

For me, I felt that I could not get enough school, because there were so many interesting things to do. In my day, we had to walk five miles to school and back. It was fun because a lot of us would be walking together.

We would sometimes stop on the way and get red clay to eat, or pick plums, huckleberries or some kind of fruit right off of the trees to eat. There were so many different kinds of fruit growing on trees on our way to school.

We also collected rocks. It was fun and something I could do that didn't cost money. I would wash them off and put them in a bowl. You can find a lot of different kinds of rocks, even rocks of different colors. They look pretty once they were washed off and put in a bowl of water. Sometimes we put them with our flowers.

I grew up and went to high school. I was looking forward to the future, planning my future, thinking about what I wanted to become in life. We still stayed very busy, but I always found time to study.

We had to study by lamplight. We had kerosene lamps, which did not give a lot of light, but it was all we had.

We lived on a big farm and my dad had a big syrup mill. The cane was planted. When it grew and got ripe, we had to cut it down, strip it and take it to the cane mill, to get the juice ground out of it. Then it was put into the big cane mill to be cooked syrup. After that, it was then put in cans or buckets and sent to the stores to be sold.

There were two kinds of syrup we made: ribbon cane syrup and sorghum syrup. We used mallets to keep the juice stirred so it would not burn, but cook into syrup. We grew a

The Better Things in Life Await You by Mary Ellen Davis

lot of vegetables. We would pick them and carry them to market. We had a big cotton farm. We picked a lot of cotton and it had to be weighed. We put it into bags to be sold. There were so many things to do to keep us busy.   We learned a lot about animals.

A Turtle

25

We had hogs and chickens. We would raise the little chicks and sell them also. We had big incubators to keep them in. We grew peanuts and all types of things.

Guess what? On the farm you learn science, math and reading. You learn science when you learn all about frogs, snakes, insects, animals, etc.

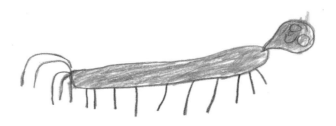

Farm Critter

On the farm, we used our math skills. You had to count things, like our chickens, cows and other animals.

Happy Chicken

27

The Better Things in Life Await You by Mary Ellen Davis

We did a lot of reading. On the farm, you have to read about plants and read the directions for different items. We also had to use math to figure out the price of our products.

Farm Fresh Corn

You learn so many things on the farm as well as in the city. You get so much experience when you are in school and go to the farm.

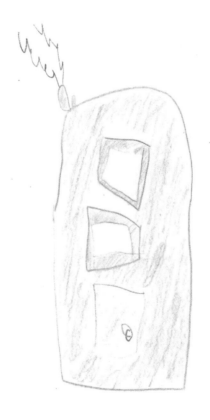

Farm House

On the farm, you get a chance to plant seeds, then harvest them. You may even get to ride horses.

Meal Time!

I always liked to read a lot. I could learn so much about people, travel, animals, different countries, languages, rivers, the Universe and all of its galaxies. I could go on and on. So, you see, it's very important that you read. It keeps us up on current events. Reading also helped me be successful in high school.

After I finished high school, I went off to college. I worked all summer to make money so I could send myself to college.

The college I went to, I had to move to the city. I was blessed to get a job at the college being a matron over the dormitory. It was good because I had a place to live where I attended school. This was nice because I could be around all of the young ladies.

The Better Things in Life Await You by Mary Ellen Davis

Later on, as I progressed in school, I learned how to be a dental assistant, and I got a job in the dentist's office, which I loved. I had to have dental work done, so that same dentist did the work. He gave me pure gold on my teeth and of course, I really liked that.

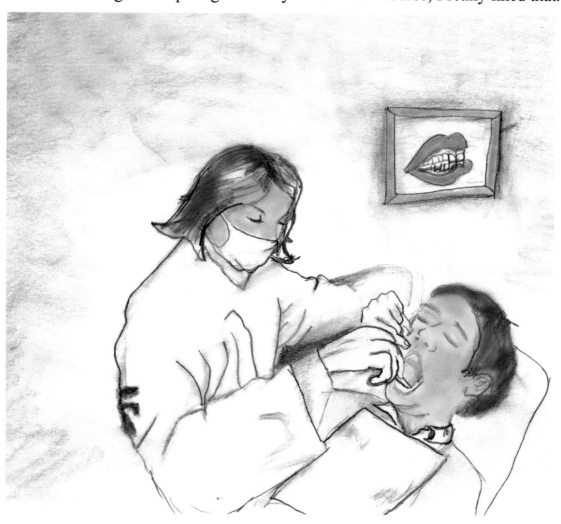

I became a member of the band while in college. I played the French horn. We played for all the football games.

I had a chance to go to so many different places. I worked hard so I could stay at the top of my classes; that's very important. Always try to keep your grades up.

I think I have told you enough about myself. I hope what I have said will enlighten your little hearts and minds to grow and make a good future for yourselves.

I have one last thing to say to you boys and girls. Learn to respect your teachers. Be obedient, be kind to one another, love your parents, follow instructions, and watch the company you keep. Keep a good attitude.

Good luck, have a real beautiful future, study hard, and don't forget to be the best you can. Later, after I retired from work, I became a Foster Grandparent, which is when I decided to write this book.

P.S. (Ann J. Kellogg, Students and Staff) I love all of you so very much. You have taught me a lot of things; working with you has kept me young at heart. I also learned a lot of things, by studying along with you. You have been an inspiration to me. I will always remember the days that I worked with boys and girls in the schools.

I like being a part of the Foster Grandparent Program in the schools. Wherever I meet you, you are always so kind and loving. This means a lot to me. I hope you enjoyed reading this little storybook, and there is more to come!

Chapter Two

Another Little Story

The Better Things in Life Await You by Mary Ellen Davis

My book will not be completed until I tell you about this young fellow I took care of from when he was just a little tot until he went into junior high school.

I would go over early in the morning, prepare his food for him and take him off to school. He was about five years old. His mother and father had to work. I would get his breakfast ready, and sing a little song about whatever he had to eat. He loved for me to sing for him. He would rush out of bed, get washed up and come and get his breakfast. I would play games with him a little before school, then help him get dressed, then off to school we would go. He hated to get up in the mornings, so we made it a fun time. He had pancakes and waffles and sausages and milk. He would tell me what he wanted for breakfast, so I could have it ready when he awoke. He was such an obedient child, lovely and respectful. He was the only child in the family, but he was one who knew how to play alone, and enjoy it. His mother trained him well. Sometimes, I would give him a treat and take him to get some food before we got to school. I loved him very much and he loved me. He loved school and his teacher.

The Better Things in Life Await You by Mary Ellen Davis

The years went by fast. One day he asked me if I would teach him how to cook, so I said yes, I would. His food had to be just like he wanted it, or he would tell you about it. He soon learned how to fix his own eggs the way he wanted them, and make his waffles and pancakes.

One morning I had him to prepare his mom and dad's eggs and toast. They were so surprised, because they didn't know I had been teaching him to cook. He was a smart youngster. He liked for his clothes to fit just right, or I would get more out for him, and tell his mother so she could get just what he wanted. He always looked so good when he went to school. He kept his body clean, wanted his hair just right, and nice shoes. He was very respectful with a wonderful attitude.

He loved to learn about everything. That young man's name was Eric. Today he is a businessman, and he is doing real well. I hated to stop caring for him, when he went to jr. high school, but it was time for him to be on his own. I am so proud of him. I will always think of him as my little boy (smile). He plays basketball and got along with other children very well. He knew how to play alone, and be happy about it. He loved to share with other boys and girls. This is something all boys and girls must learn to do; share and get along with others, have a good attitude, be obedient and respectful; this will earn you a beautiful future and life.

Life is as beautiful as we make it. Everybody needs somebody, so be kind and loving one to another. Enjoy your young life because you are only young once. Take life one day at a time, and make each day the best it can be.

Growing up is so beautiful and exciting, each day is a new challenge. Make life be the best it can be for you each day, and you can achieve your goals with joy. Boys and girls, the more you learn, the more you earn, so get to it. Learn to take what you have and make the best out of it. (By the way, this young man, Eric, received 2 four year scholarships!)

Now, there is something else important about this young man. While he was in college, during the summer months, he needed a job to help him while he was not in school. He could not find anything, so he thought about how I had taught him to make omelets, and he got a job making omelets in a restaurant for the summer.

There is something else this wonderful young man did. When Eric graduated from college, he couldn't find a job in his field so guess what? He took a job at Ann J. Kellogg School, working with the youngsters until he could find a job in his field.

So you see, boys and girls, it is important that you use all your gifts and talents and don't stop looking and searching for what you want. Never give up on your future; you can make it if you try.

The Better Things in Life Await You by Mary Ellen Davis

Chapter Three

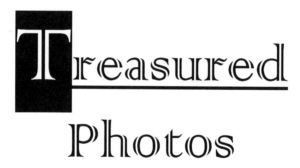

Treasured Photos

The Better Things in Life Await You by Mary Ellen Davis

The street I grew up on in Malakoff, Texas.

(Named for my father. Barron is our family name.)

Dancing and prancing about at

Great grandmother's wedding

Taking a look back…

My two grandsons

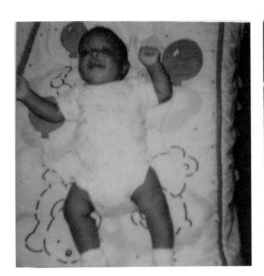

Raushawn and Rauvel Bodiford

My Son Raymond Davis

My 1st born grandson, Raushawn D. Bodiford

Me!

My Father R. David Barron

43

Eric (Then and Now)

The Better Things in Life Await You by Mary Ellen Davis

Me with my husband Simmie W. Davis, Jr.

Me and my flowers

About the Cover Artist

Anna Arnold, Director of the Florence O'Donnell Wasmer Gallery at Ursuline College in Pepper Pike, Ohio and community muralist, has been one of America's most expressive, exciting, enduring artists and independent educators for nearly three decades. She is an advocate of life-long learning and recently graduated from Case Western Reserve University School of Graduate Studies program where she earned a Master's degree in Art Education. Anna earned a Bachelor of Fine Arts degree from the Cleveland Institute of Art and has exhibited in over 200 solo and group art exhibits throughout the United States. Anna believes her work is a catalyst to inspire, uplift and change.

Additional artwork rendered by Zion D. Bodiford, Re'Zon D. Bodiford, Symone A. Bodiford, my great grandchildren.

Here is space
to write <u>your</u> story!

The Better Things in Life Await You by Mary Ellen Davis

The Better Things in Life Await You by Mary Ellen Davis

The Better Things in Life Await You by Mary Ellen Davis

The Better Things in Life Await You by Mary Ellen Davis

The Better Things in Life Await You by Mary Ellen Davis

The Better Things in Life Await You by Mary Ellen Davis

The Better Things in Life Await You by Mary Ellen Davis

The Better Things in Life Await You by Mary Ellen Davis

To Contact the Author

Mary E. Davis can be reached at:

Parablist Publishing House, Inc.

Email: parablistpublishing@yahoo.com

www.parablistbooksonline.com

Made in the USA
Charleston, SC
13 September 2014